Anointed for Work

Richard Brunton

Anointed For Work
Published by Richard Brunton
New Zealand

© 2017 Richard Brunton

First edition

ISBN 978-0-473-39612-1 (Softcover)
ISBN 978-0-473-39613-8 (ePUB)
ISBN 978-0-473-39614-5 (Kindle)

Editing:
Special thanks to
Joanne Wiklund and Andrew Killick

Production & Typesetting:
Castle Publishing Services
www.castlepublishing.co.nz

Cover design:
Paul Smith | Blue Sky Creative

International distribution by IngramSpark

CONTENTS

FOREWORD

For centuries the Holy Spirit was largely ignored in the church. Thankfully we got over that hurdle, and now at last He is being invited to take His rightful place wherever we work, wherever we go, and in our interactions with whomever we meet. Richard has found, time and again, that this kind of life is an exciting journey.

We have tended to divide life into the secular (earthly) and the sacred (heavenly), and in so doing we have shut off a valuable part of the Spirit's work. As Christians, whatever we put our hand to can be as heavenly meaningful as anything done within the walls of the church.

In this short but powerful book, Richard develops this theme and brings us to the realisation that God wants to partner with us in everything we do.

We need to get God involved in every part of our lives – at work and at home – not just at church.

John Chapter 21 tells the story of what happened when the disciples, who had struggled in their work to the point of giving up because of their lack of success, followed Jesus' advice. Having fished all night without catching a thing, the disciples were coming back to shore when Jesus called out to them from the beach and told them to cast out their nets on the right-hand side of their boat. The results were amazing. Why not find out in a very practical way how to get similar results in your place of work? I have no hesitation in commending this book to you.

Geoff Wiklund
Geoff Wiklund Ministries,
Chairman, Promise Keepers,
Auckland, New Zealand

Do you believe God has anything to say about work?

For more than two thousand years, churchmen have explored how faith might function in the lives of ordinary people. Scant centuries ago, many thought God spoke only Latin; if you needed answers to any prayer you had better find some holy, trained professional who could speak and read God's language or you could never expect help with anything. The book we call the Bible was some rare, costly, complex writing you couldn't read or afford to own, which apparently held only religious records on spiritual matters. *Really? Just how far away can we get from God's Divine life and truth?*

Thank God, the times are surely changing. And we need them to.

Sometimes it takes centuries for a hurting and disillusioned world to discover just how dumb, disappointed and damaged we have become in multiple dimensions. The time has come to return to the Divine normal and re-establish God's original purpose for us all.

Richard Brunton is a man who has found – both in his business and in fresh, breakthrough discoveries – some important biblical and practical principles that will not only show you what God is doing in the marketplace, but how He does it. Though a small and simple book, may it open for you a new way to change your world.

Winkie Pratney
Spiritual Vocations
AD 2017

INTRODUCTION

In recent years there have been some excellent books written about faith in the workplace and the idea that work is more than just a job. But as I talk to normal, everyday Christians, I've found that very few people seem to really believe and embrace that truth. Some pastors are still telling people that their primary purpose is to win souls for Christ. I just don't believe that. Winning souls is an important outcome, but it's not the primary purpose of our day-to-day lives.

I believe that the working man or woman's purpose is to do the work God has called them to do, and to do it in partnership with the Holy Spirit, in a way that glorifies Him and attracts people to the Kingdom.

This is an invitation to step into an exciting and fulfilling world, where the supernatural has a powerful impact in the workplace and in the marketplace.

As well as my own experience of 40 years in business, I have drawn from the following excellent books: *Life @Work* by John Maxwell, *Marketplace Christianity* by Robert Fraser and *Spirit-Driven Success* by Dani Johnson. I'm sure I've gleaned things from other books and people as well, but over the years it's all got merged together.

In this booklet I use the terms 'workplace' and 'marketplace'. By workplace I quite literally mean the place where you work, whether for money or not. Normally I'm thinking of a business or organisation of some kind, commercial or otherwise. But it could also be home in two senses; you may run a business from home and/or perhaps you work as a full or part-time homemaker.

The point is that although I have written mostly from my own experience in business I want to acknowledge the work that people (often women) do in the home. I believe that most of what I write applies to unpaid and/or home-based work as well.

By marketplace I mean mostly where people do business – for example a shopping mall, the dentist, the hairdresser, engaging with other businesses, and so on. The main thought here is those areas we function in outside of church-based environments.

Enjoy.

Richard Brunton

PART ONE

Foundations

THE INSIGHT

A few years ago I was interviewed at a breakfast function for Christian businessmen. Every month, the organiser, Martin Kelderman, would invite someone to be interviewed, and that month it was my turn. Martin and I sat up the front on two stools facing the audience.

Everything was going along nicely until – and I can't remember what provoked it – I began talking about the fact that, as a Christian businessman, I felt like a second-class Christian because I wasn't in full-time ministry. I felt completely insignificant in the Kingdom of Heaven – like a wallet or source of funds, engaged in the 'worthless' in order to give to the 'worthy'. This feeling had been growing inside me, hidden in my heart, but I had never voiced it. In fact, I had never properly formulated it in my conscious mind, and as I began to share my thoughts, something broke deep in me and I began to sob uncontrollably … to this day

I don't know whether it was my own personal grief or the grief of the Holy Spirit, or both.

In the conversation afterwards, I found that a lot of people in the audience felt the same way. I even had a pastor ask my forgiveness on behalf of the wider Church for what had been done to cause me to feel that way.

So, why did I feel that way? Where did these feelings come from? What messages were the churches sending out and what message was I receiving?

I recently caught up with a retired Christian CEO. He talked about an experience he'd had at a Christian gathering years earlier when a prophet stopped in front of him and said, *'Don't regard business or administration as a second-class ministry,'* before moving on to the next person.

In all my years of churchgoing I had never seen work or business truly honoured. No pastor ever said, for example, that he felt an anointing for tradesmen, business leaders, homemakers, anything like that.

But there were always anointings or impartations for other things: 'spiritual' things like soul-winning, missions, giving and other church-centric activities.

I have read several books about faith in the workplace since that day, and I have discovered that what I felt is widespread. It's wrong that it should be this way! I've even wondered if perhaps it is the reason why men are generally less likely to go to church than women; what does religion have to offer the working man?

So I want to paint a picture of what I believe is God's true plan for our work and how we – both pastors and non-church workers – can take hold of His direction.

GOD'S PLAN FOR WORK

The first thing to realise is that work is God-ordained and that it held that status before the Fall. Work is not the result of sin. Work may have become more difficult and stressful after the Fall, but it is, and always has been, a divine assignment. God created us for work.

Work is where and how we exercise the gifts God has given us:
- to reveal His glory;
- to steward, or tend to, His creation;
- to know the joy and satisfaction of co-labouring and co-creating with Him;
- to serve others;
- and to thereby make the world a better place.

God Himself is a worker. As is Jesus. In John Chapter 17 verse 4 Jesus prays to His Father,

*"I brought glory to You here on Earth
by completing the work You gave Me to do."*

The second important point is that the word 'minister' comes from a Latin word meaning 'to serve' – so ministry is *service*. For most of us, our God-given ministries (our God-given callings to serve others) are in the marketplace or in the home. A few of us are called to serve in the church, but most of us are called to serve elsewhere. I want you to see that the space outside the walls of the church (whether that be the marketplace or home) is where *most* of us are called to serve; it's the primary environment in which we seek to make the world a better place, and it's where we are called to live out and demonstrate the Kingdom of God.

If this is true, then it follows that marketplace and home *ministries* are no less valid than those of a pastor or full-time missionary. The work a plumber does, if he does it 'as unto the Lord' (Colossians 3:23), is no less approved by God than that of a pastor, or even Mother Theresa for that matter. Think about that for a moment and let it sink in. If work is indeed a God-given calling, then it follows that there is an anointing and equipping for it, just as there is for any other ministry.

That's the heart of the message of what I want you to receive and experience as you read this book. I also want to show you what I've learnt about partnering with God in the workplace and in the marketplace.

THE CONSEQUENCES OF A WRONG PERSPECTIVE

Many Christian businesspeople see work as a necessary evil – something they have to endure in order to earn money so they can do the important 'spiritual' things. I believe that this misunderstanding grieves the heart of God.

Many Christians would be known for being honest, likeable people in the workplace, but unfortunately they may not be known for their excellence. Excellence is fundamental to who God is. In Psalm 139:14 the psalmist says, 'Marvellous are Your works'. Just look at His creation! God loves skilfully made things and things of beauty. Excellence is important in our work simply because we are made in His image.

I think we can assume that Jesus was a skilled craftsman. The Bible says that 'Jesus increased in wisdom and stature and in favour with God and man' (Luke 2:52).

As a carpenter, I believe that the furniture Jesus made was not mediocre; it would have reflected the love, creativity and excellence of God.

But the message of the church to furniture-makers today is mostly around developing good character. I think it should be about making better tables, as well as working on good character. God delights in a beautiful piece of furniture made by one of His children.

A family once came to see me with concerns about their son. He was so involved in church activities that he was neglecting his university work. The son didn't realise that his studies were no less spiritual than all the church stuff he was involved with. I was able to straighten him out! (He went on to do well both spiritually and professionally.)

The excellence of your work gets you noticed, gets you promoted, gets you respected and gives you a voice. Proverbs 22:29 puts it this way:

> *Do you see a man who excels in his work?*
> *He will stand before kings;*
> *he will not stand before unknown men.*

And in Daniel 6:1-3, we read:

> *Daniel distinguished himself*
> *… because an excellent spirit was in him.*

Excellence gives you influence. It gives you the 'right' to evangelise. Mediocrity, on the other hand, earns a less favourable response: 'If he's a Christian, Christianity is not for me; I don't want to be like him!' Who you are, and what you do, speak more loudly than what you say.

If we have a wrong perspective about work, then we will miss out on the experience of partnering with the Holy Spirit; in fact, we won't even know that partnering with God is possible. In my case, a wrong understanding of God's plan for work resulted in feelings of disappointment, sadness, guilt and condemnation. It was only relatively late in my working life that I began to understand the truth and enter into what God had for me. I have always worked hard, and I was a good and successful leader, but I could have accomplished more, and done so more efficiently. A wrong perspective denies us of the joy and satisfaction of co-labouring and co-creating with God – a privilege reserved for Christians.

I should mention two other types of Christian workers I have met. The first is the lazy or misguided person who leaves everything to God. If you apply for a job and haven't taken the trouble to find out something about your future employer, you don't deserve to get the job. Focus on what you can do for the *employer*, rather than what the employer can do for *you*. By the same token, if you are competing with a non-Christian for a promotion, and you pray about it, leave it to God, then go back to the TV, while the non-Christian does the extra work and necessary study for the new position, who do think will get the promotion?

The second type of Christian worker is the other extreme. Their every thought and action on the job springs from relying completely on themselves, working independently of the Holy Spirit, because there is a basic lack of trust in God, a sense of pride or because there is no awareness that God wants to come alongside and help. These people are robbing themselves of the joy, satisfaction, creativity and efficiency of partnering with Him.

WORK CAN BE WORSHIP TOO

God created work as a way to worship Him and reveal His glory in and through His children. It's *how* you do it and what you *put into it* that makes a difference …

> *And whatever you do, do it heartily, as to the Lord and not to men … (Colossians 3:23).*

Years ago I was painting inside a wardrobe at a rental property. I was painting the parts no one would see, lying on the floor listening to Rhema, a Christian radio station. Suddenly I felt the presence of God come over me, like a divine cuddle. It was like God was saying, 'I love you, Richard. I see what you're doing even though no one else does or will. You're a man after my own heart. If you commit to excellence with a small, invisible thing, I will trust you with something bigger.'

On one occasion I was in a toilet block at an airport – I think it was in Kuala Lumpur. There was a man there in a white coat, who was in charge of this domain. Everything was immaculate. I don't know if he was a Christian or not, but to me it appeared that he was doing his work not just for ordinary men, but as if the King of Kings was going to use the toilets.

Work becomes worship when we decide to give our best every day for the good of those around us.

If any of what I said in this section speaks to you, then pray with me:

> *Heavenly Father, release me from wrong percep-tions about work and all their consequences. Rewire me, Lord. Grant me a greater revelation of your purposes for work and change my atti-tudes to align with Yours. In Jesus' name. Amen.*

Let's pause a moment. If you regularly do the bare minimum in your work rather than striving for excel-lence; if you only paint the bits that people can see; if you work grudgingly; then I call on you to repent. If I'm speaking to you, then pray with me:

Lord, I repent of my attitude to work, that I haven't regularly given my best. With your help, Holy Spirit, I commit to excellence, to honour God, and to honour myself and those I serve. In Jesus' name. Amen.

THE ANOINTING AND EQUIPPING FOR WORK

As I said earlier, if work is a God-given calling then it follows that we can be anointed and equipped for it, just as a pastor would be. Potentially, this includes an additional spiritual dimension unavailable to non-Christians. If we are diligent to turn our natural talents into skills and submit them to God, then He will add something more in order to accomplish the work He has uniquely called us to do. What we produce as a result will bring admiration from others and give glory to God. This is the underlying message that comes through in Exodus 31:1–11:

> Then the Lord spoke to Moses, saying: 'See, I have called by name Bezalel the son of Uri, the son of Hur, of the tribe of Judah. And I have filled him with the Spirit of God, in wisdom, in understanding, in knowledge, and in all manner of workmanship, to design artistic works, to work

in gold, in silver, in bronze, in cutting jewels for setting, in carving wood, and to work in all manner of workmanship.

'And I, indeed I, have appointed with him Aholiab the son of Ahisamach, of the tribe of Dan; and I have put wisdom in the hearts of all the gifted artisans, that they may make all that I have commanded you: the tabernacle of meeting, the ark of the Testimony and the mercy seat that is on it, and all the furniture of the tabernacle – the table and its utensils, the pure gold lampstand with all its utensils, the altar of incense, the altar of burnt offering with all its utensils, and the laver and its base – the garments of ministry, the holy garments for Aaron the priest and the garments of his sons, to minister as priests, and the anointing oil and sweet incense for the holy place. According to all that I have commanded you they shall do.'

I believe that it's reasonable to infer from this scripture that God will give a *skilled worker* extra skill, beyond his or her natural ability, to accomplish God's

Kingdom purposes in the worker's craft and life.

I think we can personalise this scripture:

> *'See, I have called you by name (put your own name here) and I have filled you with the Spirit of God, in wisdom, in understanding, in knowledge and in all manner of workmanship, in particular (put your own particular skill in here), that you may accomplish all that I have purposed for you to do.'*

(By the way, if you have a natural talent and you haven't developed it into skill, then, well, you know what you have to do!)

Notice that the Holy Spirit *knows* how to do practical work. In the same way as He had the craftsmanship for decorating the temple, He knows how to do plumbing, medicine, toilet cleaning, aircraft engineering, marketing research, home-making and accounting ... Because He is all-knowing and created our world, He knows how to do these things brilliantly, way beyond our natural ability.

Have you ever thought about the Holy Spirit like that before?

He is more than willing to impart skills, ideas and new thinking if we meet His conditions. This is an aspect of the infilling of the Holy Spirit for everyday life that is seldom talked about – in fact, I've never heard anyone talk about it. When God calls, He qualifies, He equips and He prepares. When a Christian is called to a new responsibility, he or she needs to be equipped, regardless of whether that calling is in the church, the marketplace or at home. Hence, a Christian needs to be anointed by the Holy Spirit as God provides what the Christian needs in order to fulfil his or her new and unique calling (see also Daniel 1:17–20).

Let's release the power and presence of God into our workplaces, not just to share the gospel, or to model good character, but also to glorify Him with our talents and skills.

I wish a pastor, or wise Christian businessman, had prayed for me for the impartation of Godly wisdom, knowledge and skill for my craft and calling (marketing research). How wonderful that would have been!

I once shared my thoughts on this subject with the pastor of a large church. During a Sunday service, not long afterwards, he asked me to stand and pray for the businesspeople in the congregation. I briefly prayed for a 'workplace anointing' to fall on those who stood to receive it. It was a powerful moment that had a long-lasting impact. A few months later, I had the opportunity to do something similar with around 1,500 men, and again the impact was very noticeable. Since then I have seen many instances of the Holy Spirit being only too willing to release a workplace anointing.

The Holy Spirit wants to help believers in their daily work just as much as when they contribute at church. He wants to come alongside us at the office, on the building site, in the home, or wherever our workplace is. He wants to input His know-how, and take our level of skill to heights that it would otherwise be impossible for us to reach. But we must trust Him. It is up to us to ask for His help. It is our choice – to yield our skills to Him or to continue to work on our own. Is this an exciting proposition, or what?

Let's look at it another way: doesn't it make a difference when we worship with the help of Holy Spirit? As we surrender ourselves to Him, and worship in the Spirit, He takes us right into the throne room of God – a wonderful example of partnering with the Holy Spirit. In the same way, as we surrender our workplace skills to Him, He will add love, inspiration, creativity and beauty to our workplace offering. I believe that God takes great delight in this partnership. After all, we were created by Him for joy and intimacy.

A PRAYER FOR A WORKPLACE ANOINTING

To receive an anointing for the workplace, I think the ideal is that a pastor, with a love and respect for your calling, lays hands on you and prays. Otherwise, a wise Christian businessperson or homemaker, who has experienced partnering with Holy Spirit, can lay hands on you for impartation. If neither of these options are possible or practical, you can pray the following prayer slowly: tailoring it to your situation in a sincere worshipful way,

Dear Father, please anoint me and equip me for the workplace and the marketplace. Fill me with Your Holy Spirit, in wisdom, in understanding, in knowledge and in all manner of workmanship for that which You have called me to do.

Holy Spirit, please add love and creativity and beauty to all that I do, and may my work bring

fresh joy and satisfaction to You and to me. May my work bring You glory, Lord.

May I grow in influence and so advance Your Kingdom, Lord.

I hereby declare myself commissioned and sent forth to be a home or marketplace minister. I go in the power of the Holy Spirit. In Jesus' name. Amen.

Please take your time over this prayer and let the significance of it sink in. Repeat it if necessary. Activate your faith and receive the anointing intentionally.

RAISING OUR SIGHTS FURTHER

I love what Os Hillman wrote as a word from the Lord in his book *Listening to the Father's Heart*:

> *Son, if you want to have influence in the lives of others and your community, and even your nation, you must be a source of blessing. You must solve problems where there appear to be no solutions. When my Son's disciples needed food for the 5,000, He simply instructed them to give them something to eat. They looked at their five loaves and two fish and were bewildered, understanding His instruction only from their natural mind. He was trying to get them to think beyond their experiences and use the power He had demonstrated to them. Each of my sons and daughters has a latent power within them to solve societal problems. When they tap into that power, people witness my glory and are drawn*

to Me and My Son. Every time you learn of a problem, ask me how I might want to solve that problem through you.

ANOINTING FOR A PROMOTION OR A CHANGE IN OCCUPATION

We have talked about *occupations*, for example being a plumber, schoolteacher, homemaker and so on. But what about *roles and positions* within our occupations, or even changing occupations so that we are better utilising our talents and skills?

Imagine I am promoted to be a supervisor or a leader. Should I then seek a leadership anointing? I believe so. Effectively, this is humbling oneself before God (a bit like Solomon did in 1 Kings 3:6–9) and saying: *'Come, Holy Spirit. Anoint me and help me to serve and grow the people I am now responsible for. In Jesus' name. Amen.'* However, I believe it will mark the occasion more intentionally to have a pastor or an experienced leader do this for you. Seek a prayer of anointing whenever you step into positions of greater responsibility or potential.

ANOINTING FOR UNPAID ROLES IN THE HOME

Many of us do unpaid work in the home – in very important roles, such as mother/father or grandmother/grandfather. In hindsight, I wish I had been anointed for these roles when I first stepped into them. I'm sure I would have been a much better father and grandfather if I had.

Within the church, the work of anointing individuals for different occupations, promotions and roles can be shared – it doesn't have to be left to the pastor alone. There are many people sitting on the sidelines of church who have great wisdom and experience that is going to waste. An experienced Christian business leader, for example, could anoint a newly promoted man or woman for leadership; or an experienced mother or father could anoint a new mother or father and encourage them. Not everyone wants to be involved in praying for healing and deliverance, or other needs, but many might be interested in this ministry of anointing others.

PART TWO:

Working in the Spirit

INTRODUCTION

Having better understood the anointing and equipping of the Holy Spirit, let's move on to another question. What is the difference between a Christian worker and a non-Christian worker?

The simple answer is that one has the Holy Spirit, and the other doesn't. One carries the presence of God, and the other doesn't. If there are 100 people in a workplace and five percent are Christians, then those five people bring the Holy Spirit into the workplace.

Think about that for a moment. *We carry the Holy Spirit into the workplace!* And, what's more, He wants out – He's waiting for us to release Him. It's our privilege and responsibility to activate the Kingdom of God in the workplace.

The outcome of taking the Holy Spirit into the workplace can be far-reaching, but I want to talk about four potential effects:

- Co-labouring/co-creating with God
- Spiritual authority in the workplace
- The fruit of the Spirit in the workplace
- The gifts of the Spirit in the workplace and marketplace

CO-LABOURING/CO-CREATING WITH THE HOLY SPIRIT IN THE WORKPLACE

Imagine a scene like this: One day a son goes around to help in his father's garden. Without knocking on the door, he immediately goes under the house, gets the mower out and starts it up. His dad hears the noise, gets out of his armchair, goes outside onto the balcony and waves to attract his son's attention. The son stops what he's doing and comes over.

'What is it, Dad?'
'Son, come in and have a cup of tea and a chat, then we'll go and do the garden together.'
Most of us are like the son. We concentrate on the task, sometimes forgetting the relationship. The son had good intentions, but went to work in his own strength. Could he finish the job by himself? Of course. But even in the physical realm, two can accomplish more than one. Our Heavenly

Father wants to work with us. Imagine the joy and sense of camaraderie the father and son will have accomplishing something together. That's why God made us. We can experience some of what it was like in the Garden of Eden when He and Adam enjoyed that level of closeness.

Gordon Richards is the managing director of an industrial cleaning business. He writes:

Over the last 33 years I've been continually amazed how God has guided and blessed my business.

Many years ago, I invited Him to be my Managing Director. He has always been there, available any time, in everyday work situations. While it's great that God's there to help in the big stuff, I'm continually blessed in the smaller details, for example a different way of doing a particular job. 'Thanks Holy Spirit, what a great idea,' I'd say, then I'd do it His way and find it most often took less effort and the finished work always looked much better!

In 2011, I wrote down a word I received from God. When I say I 'received and wrote it down', I mean I put into words the impression I felt in my spirit. I believe He was saying to me:

> *I created you for My pleasure,*
> *That you would know Me and love Me;*
> *And I have given you work to do,*
> *For the service of others,*
> *And for your joy and satisfaction.*
> *Your greatest joy comes from working with Me,*
> *By co-creating with Me.*
> *Therefore, involve Me in all your work,*
> *In all its details,*
> *And I will bless your work,*
> *And thereby also those you serve,*
> *And men will see Me in you.*

It's absolutely true that God wants to be involved in our work and all its details. But if we don't know this, then we will have no expectation – we won't even ask.

One of my greatest joys comes when Almighty God inspires me with a clever idea. It's so exciting. On one occasion, I wrote an article for the *Sunday Star Times*. My whole life message for business was encapsulated in that article, but it took only 10 minutes to write! I had got into the Holy Spirit flow. The PR people didn't change a word, which was very unusual! A much respected company director rang me a few days after the article was published to say it was brilliant – absolutely spot on – and told me he was going to show it to his son. I give God the glory for the message He gave me, and for helping me to communicate it so clearly.

If we work independently of God, we rob Him of joy and satisfaction. Have you ever thought of it that way? And we rob ourselves of the same thing. But it makes sense doesn't it? After all, God created us for intimacy and to enjoy Him. If we don't take hold of this truth, then we also rob the world of what God desires to release through us.

Consider King David, known as a man after God's own heart. Time and again, the books of Samuel tell us that David 'inquired of the Lord'. He sought God for everything he did, and God gave him the victory every time.

Sometimes we find ourselves in situations where we need to pray:

> *Holy Spirit, please help me with this problem. I'm so confused, I don't know where to start and the work's due tomorrow. Lord, grant me clarity and peace. Lord, let me have your mind. I receive it now in Jesus' name. Thank you, thank you Lord. Amen.*

Having prayed this prayer, wait for a moment, and then just start your project.

If we're good at what we do, it's easy to operate out of our own strength. In which case, perhaps we need to pray:

> *Holy Spirit, I know I can do a pretty good job of this in my own strength. Thank you for the talents You've given me. But I want to create*

something wonderful with You, Lord. Grant me the joy of working with You – You and I together. Let's add love and creativity and beauty into this project. In Jesus' name I release your genius. I release the mind of Christ. Amen.

So, how do we tune in to the flow of the Holy Spirit? *We talk to Him about everything.* I know this isn't easy; in the beginning it takes practice. I am writing this as much for myself as for you, the reader. I often forget, but I get better day by day. It's all about learning a new habit. God is patient with us. Time and again we've gone off on our own tangent. But He is faithful to forgive us and we can pray:

Lord we confess we have failed to share the details of our work lives with You, and in doing so we have robbed both You and ourselves. We repent Lord. We want to be men and women after Your own heart. Help us Holy Spirit. Keep drawing us to Yourself. As a magnet always seeks north, so help us to look afresh to You when we forget. In Jesus' name. Amen.

I find that writing to God helps me communicate with Him; then I write down what I believe He says in return. While working on this book, and thinking about our partnership with God, I asked what He would like to say to you, the reader. Here's what He said:

> *Tell them that I love them, Richard, and I long to have an intimate relationship with them. Of course your enemy and your old nature does not want that and you will face many distractions. But believe Me when I say that the prize is worth way more than the effort. All the great saints have mastered this and so can you if you desire it and pursue it strongly enough. It won't just happen. It will take huge effort in the beginning but everything else will become easier.*

SPIRITUAL AUTHORITY IN THE WORKPLACE

One day, I was sitting on Ouen Toro, a lookout point in Noumea, seeking a message to bring to a prayer group that I was involved with. I sensed God say, *'You don't know who you are.'* Then some months later, *'If you only knew the authority you have in Christ Jesus you would change the world.'* Both of these messages were for particular groups of people but, I realised later, they were for me too.

These messages made me realise the significance and implications of something I had discovered earlier but had never thought all the way through. I talk about this in my book *The Awesome Power of Blessing* (available as a free download from www.thepowerofblessing.com), but it applies here too. Some years ago, I started the practice of going to work early to bless my business (the market research company, Colmar Brunton).

At first I simply said, 'God, bless Colmar Brunton.' It felt flat. So I changed my words – a little timidly at first – from 'God bless Colmar Brunton' to 'Colmar Brunton, I bless you in the name of the Father, the Son and the Holy Spirit.' Eventually the blessing became something like this:

Colmar Brunton, I bless you in the name of the Father, the Son and the Holy Spirit.

I bless you in Auckland, and I bless you in Wellington, and I bless you in the regions. I bless you at work and I bless you at home. I release the Kingdom of God in this place.

Come Holy Spirit, You are welcome here.

I release love and joy and peace and patience and kindness and goodness and gentleness and faithfulness and self-control and unity.

In the name of Jesus, I release ideas from the Kingdom of God that would help our clients succeed and make the world a better place.

I release favour in the client marketplace. I release favour in the employment marketplace.
I bless our vision: Better Business, Better World. In Jesus' name. Amen.

From the moment I changed my words from 'God, bless Colmar Brunton' to 'Colmar Brunton, I bless you in the name of the Father, the Son and the Holy Spirit', the anointing of God fell on me; I felt God's pleasure and affirmation. It was like He was saying, 'You've got it, son; that's what I want you to do.' So what was the difference? At first, I was praying a passive prayer. But I moved from there into acting out of the authority God had given me, giving a blessing that flowed from the Holy Spirit living in me. Though I must have done this now hundreds of times, I've always felt God's pleasure in it.

And the results of that blessing? The atmosphere in the office changed, and changed rapidly, to the point where people would comment on it, and wonder why things were so different. It really was amazing! Blessing can change our world.

I think it is generally known in Christian circles that speaking directly to a disease or condition and commanding a healing is more effective than asking God to do it (Matthew 10:8; Mark 16:17–18). This has certainly been my experience, and the experience of many other well-known and respected people in the healing and deliverance ministry. I believe that Jesus says in effect, '*You* heal the sick (in My name). It's not *My* job, it's *your* job. *You* do it.'

I have concluded that:
- God wants to heal, and He wants to do it through us.
- God wants to deliver, and He wants to do it through us.
- God wants to bless, and He wants to do it through us.

Eventually I extended my practice of blessing the workplace more widely. In the morning, before anyone else arrived at the Colmar Brunton office, I would make my way through the workspace. When I came to the chair of someone who needed wisdom for a particular situation, I would bless them, laying hands on their chair, believing that an anointing to accomplish the blessing would pass into the fabric of the chair and so onto the person when they arrived at work (Acts 19:12). Whenever I was aware of specific needs that people were facing, I would bless them accordingly.

I particularly remember one man who habitually used God's name as an expletive. One morning I laid my hands on his chair, binding the spirit of blasphemy, in Jesus' name. It took several attempts, but eventually the evil spirit behind his foul language had to bow the knee to a greater power, and blasphemy disappeared from the man's workplace vocabulary.

On one occasion, a man came to me for prayer, wanting God to take him out of his place of work because blasphemy was common there. I persuaded him otherwise: God had placed him in that position so that he could bless his workplace and change the atmosphere!

As I felt led, I would make a sign of the cross at the entrance to Colmar Brunton and spiritually apply the protection of the blood of Jesus over our business. We are naïve if we think there are not evil forces aligned against Christian businesses.

Jesus has given us spiritual authority and asks us to use it. Our Heavenly Father wants us to *participate* – to *co-labour* – with Him in His redemptive work. What a privilege and responsibility! When we bless our businesses and speak God's intentions and favour over them, we release His ability to change things from where they are to where He wants them to be.

A word of caution: Blessing is not some kind of magic spell. For example, God will not make people buy what they don't need or want. Nor will He bless laziness and dishonesty. But if we work for Him diligently and utilise the power of blessing, God will help you to take your business to greater levels. Listen for His counsel or the counsel of the people He sends to you. Be open, and expect His favour, because He loves you and wants you to succeed.

I received the following testimony from Ben Fox:

My particular role in the property industry underwent some changes and there was a significant downturn in my business. I had gone to several people asking for prayer for my job because my workload was declining to the point where I was worried and anxious.

About the same time, in early 2015, I heard Mr Brunton preach a series of messages about blessing one's job, business, family and other areas. Until that time, the focus of my prayers had been to ask God to help me in these areas. The idea of speaking a blessing for ourselves had not been taught to me, but I can now see that the concept is found in the Bible, and I know God calls us, and has given us the authority, to do so in the name of Jesus. So I started to bless my work – to speak the word of God over it and to thank God for it. I persisted with this blessing each morning and also thanked God for new business, asking Him to send me clients I could help.

Over the next twelve months, my work volume increased significantly and, since then, I have sometimes been hard-pressed to handle the amount of work that has come my way. I have learned that there is a way to include God in our everyday lives, and blessing our work is part of what God calls us to do. I therefore give God all the credit. I also began to invite the Holy Spirit into my workday, asking for wisdom and creative ideas. In particular, I have noticed that when I ask the Holy Spirit to help me with the efficiency of my work, I usually finish it well before the expected time.

Blessing my work has now become a daily habit, as has blessing others. I look forward with expectation to seeing the fruit in the people and the things I bless when it is in accordance with God's word and in Jesus' name.

The story of blessing Colmar Brunton was told from my point of view as a business owner and leader. But what if you are an employee in a business owned by someone else? I still strongly recommend that you bless that business, and bless those higher up the chain of authority. You will find that your relationship with the organisation and your boss or manager will undergo a positive change. By blessing your workplace, you will position yourself for God's favour and promotion. Just do it!

What if your place of work is your home? Blessing the place where you live simply involves using your spiritual authority in Christ Jesus to dedicate and consecrate that place to the Lord. It invites the Holy Spirit to come, and compels everything else that is not of God to leave.

A home is not just bricks and mortar; it has personality too. Just as you now have legal access to your house and property (as the owner or tenant), someone else had legal access to it before you. Things may have happened in that place that brought either blessings or curses. No matter what has happened there in the past, it is *your* authority that determines what the spiritual atmosphere will be like from now on. If there is demonic activity going on from past ownership, you will likely sense it – and it is up to you to drive those forces out.

Of course, you have to consider what demonic forces *you* may be unwittingly giving access to your home. Do you have ungodly paintings, artefacts, books, music or DVDs? What TV programmes do you or other family members watch? Is there sin in your home?

Here is a simple blessing you could make as you walk through your house room by room:

I bless this house, our home. I declare that this house belongs to God, I consecrate it to Him and place it under the Lordship of Jesus Christ. It is a house of blessing.

I break every curse in this house with the blood of Jesus. I take authority over any and every demon in Jesus' name and I command them to leave now and never to return. I cast out every spirit of strife, division and discord. I cast out the spirit of poverty.

Come Holy Spirit and evict everything that is not of you. Fill this house with your presence. Let your fruit come: love, joy, peace, kindness, patience, goodness, gentleness, faithfulness and self-control. I bless this house with overflowing peace and abounding love. May all who come here sense your presence and be blessed. In Jesus' name. Amen.

In the same way, if you have school-age children, you can place your hands on them and say something like this:

Johnny, I bless you in Jesus' name. May the love of God surround you and fill you. May His angels protect you. I bless you to be healthy and strong. I bless you with good friends. I bless you with a love of learning – to understand your lessons, particularly (subject) … I bless the gifts that God has placed inside you to develop and grow. I love you Johnny. Have a great day at school.

And of course, you can bless the main income-earner, that he or she would be sensitive to the promptings of the Holy Spirit, and that the Holy Spirit would add love, beauty and creativity to his or her work.

THE FRUIT OF THE SPIRIT IN THE WORKPLACE

When we take the Holy Spirit to work, the fruit of the Spirit come with Him: love, joy, peace, patience, kindness, goodness, faithfulness, gentleness and self-control.

I co-founded Colmar Brunton in 1981, and became a born-again Christian three years later in 1984. So I have had a before and after experience – I know the difference that being a Christian made to my business life.

When I was born again and filled with the Spirit, the biggest change for me was how much more I loved people and I brought that love to work. Over the next 30 years, that love became evident in a number of different ways.

I became kinder, more generous, more considerate and more patient. I remember one occasion when I was sitting with a group of employees at Eden Park, watching a Rugby World Cup game. Before kick-off, the wife of an employee approached me to say how grateful she was about the way we had handled a sensitive situation regarding her husband. I had many compliments like that over the years, and they came about because I cared for the people I worked with.

But perhaps the biggest manifestation of love in the workplace was the enjoyment I gained from *identifying and developing people's gifts* – calling forth their potential, helping them find their greatness. I am truly amazed at how people thrive when we release them into their potential. At our conferences I would see researchers who were poets, dancers, singers, composers, musicians, painters, visionaries and innovators – talents that were part of who these employees really were.

We developed a culture of recognition – we actively appreciated, valued, praised and celebrated people's gifts or strengths. I would look for the gold in people, not the dirt. What is fascinating is that when we draw out and celebrate the gold, the dirt tends to reduce by itself!

It's so important to know your greatness (the talents and identity that you hold as a child of God) and help the people around you find theirs. When you've figured out your own strengths, and the strengths of the people around you, work on those abilities – invest in them and enhance them even further. We tend to do the opposite. Instead of honing our natural strengths, we strive to fill in the gaps. If you spend your life trying to be good at everything, you'll never be great at anything.

In general, I would rather employ someone who is outstanding at something than someone who is merely good at everything, because I can turn that 'outstandingness' into a competitive advantage in the marketplace.

I worked out a long time ago that I am a big-picture person; I'm impatient with detail. But detail is important. The point is, I could battle to become better at detail or I could invest in my strengths to become outstanding and hire somebody who is gifted and enthusiastic about the things I'm not.

If you want to grow your business (or church for that matter) you need to progress from being a star, to being a *star-maker*. I learned to let go of my own individual glory and release the glory in others. I went from being a single candle, to being the light at the base of a chandelier that was full of candles. That chandelier became my glory, my legacy. Sadly, many people struggle to let go of their own glory, and never experience the rewards of letting others shine.

People need to feel that their work is *significant,* that it has meaning and makes the world a better place. With this in mind, if you're a business leader, state your mission in terms of making your customers' lives better.

At Colmar Brunton we represented the consumer in the boardrooms of New Zealand, aiming to convince businesses that they would create more shareholder value if they genuinely focused on delivering a great customer experience. Our slogan was Better Business, Better World.

All these things came about as a result of bringing the Holy Spirit to work. They are all examples of the evidence of the fruit of the Spirit, and the *outworking* of love. This is wisdom that has come from the Spirit over the course of more than 30 years. I share it in the hope that young executives will pick up where I left off.

When in business, profit, budgeting and cashflow are very important. Sometimes love and profit can be in tension but, in general, I have found them to be excellent partners.

Apart from love, the other big change that developed when I became a Christian was around holiness and integrity.

Financial integrity is vital. Most big companies have appropriate systems in place and a code of conduct that addresses such things as bribes, gifts and personal expenses. But for a smaller operator, there will be a temptation to classify personal expenses as business ones. God won't bless a situation like that.

He also won't bless such things as gossip. God detests that. Don't speak evil of other people. Then there's exaggeration or lying when attempting to make a sale, or taking the credit for someone else's work. And so on. Tune in to your Spirit-led conscience, and do what's right.

Who you are and what you *do* speak more loudly than what you say. On Sunday, or at a church prayer group, you can be Mr or Mrs Nice, but it's more difficult to put on a mask in the workplace where people see you day in and day out. There's no point just talking about the gospel, we actually have to *be* the message.

GIFTS OF THE SPIRIT IN THE WORKPLACE

George O. Wood, the General Superintendent of the Assemblies of God in the United States, makes an excellent point about the gifts of the Spirit as listed in 1 Corinthians 12:

> One thing about the gifts is perhaps surprising: only a few of them occur in a church service. If you look carefully at the gifts of the Spirit as they occur in the Book of Acts, the gifts mostly occur in the marketplace. The majority of them occur in everyday service to Christ or in the functioning of the Body outside of the worship service, in ministry to the world. In the workplace – at work and for work.

Does it come as a shock or surprise to you that the Holy Spirit would move in the workplace? Perhaps you think the Holy Spirit is only supposed to be doing 'spiritual stuff' – preferably in a church building or prayer group. But as we have seen, your work *is* your spiritual stuff!

Know that the Holy Spirit is very interested in your work, then ask and expect.

I have actively seen the gifts of revelation and discernment in my working life. On many occasions I have heard myself say things that were so good I felt that I should have written them down; such things come from the Holy Spirit. I've had what I call 'flashes of wisdom', and once had a tagline for a brand dropped into my mind by God. If I had known when I was younger that this was possible, I would have been alert, asking and expecting, much earlier in my career.

Some revelations can be truly amazing. I have read and heard of people receiving formulas and designs given to them by the Holy Spirit. I haven't personally received anything as dramatic as that, but it does happen. We should ask for these things, and expect to receive them.

I think it's worth repeating the words from Os Hillman that were quoted earlier:

> *Each of My sons and daughters has a latent power within them to solve societal problems. When they tap into that power, people witness My glory and are drawn to Me and My Son. Every time you learn of a problem, ask Me how I might want to solve that problem through you.*

Here are a few testimonies of the gifts of the Spirit in operation in the workplace. Be encouraged and inspired. Expect more.

> *I mostly work alone so I talk to God about all sorts of things. One day it was raining and I was working outside, clearing along a boundary. All was well and I only had a few metres to go when I uncovered a large concrete slab. I instantly knew I wouldn't be able to lift it. I said to God, 'Well, I did agree to clear all the rubbish and you're the God who keeps your word, and I know that You expect me to keep my word also, so I need Your help.' I moved my trailer close to the slab, and*

said, 'How?' The Holy Spirit said, 'Place one hand either side.' Before I knew it, the slab was on top of the load! I didn't stop praising God all the way to the tip. When I arrived, I wondered, 'Okay. How to get it off again?' So I placed one hand on top and one under and, with no effort, shifted it end over end, off the trailer onto the concrete floor. The attendant came over because the slab shook the building as it landed. He looked at the slab then at me and his mouth fell open. I was so excited – I gave God the glory all the way home and still do.

Roger Samsom *(Builder)*

I was called to a business where some serious theft was taking place. There were cameras in place but they hadn't been able to catch the person who was getting away with huge amounts of stock. Each new effort had brought no result and hence the call for a pastor! I went in and prayed.

After I prayed, God identified the person by telling me what he looked like and where he stood as he watched the girls serving. From the description and location, the owner immediately knew who the person was and was shocked. He was the storeman who ordered and controlled the stock, and of course he had access to the surveillance equipment. Having identified 'who', the business owners were then able to work out the 'when' and the 'how'. The next evening, a very surprised storeman (who had covertly removed some stock and hidden it behind a bank outside) was met by a couple of large policemen when he later returned with a trailer to make the collection.

On another occasion, a businessman asked me to come and pray over a dilemma he was facing. He needed to borrow a large sum of money to expand his businesses but was about to face competition from another business opening up right next door. Because he had already borrowed for a new house, he would lose everything if his business failed. As I prayed, I heard myself say to the man that in a year's time he would increase his takings by 25 percent. He showed me the figures for other similar businesses and no one was doing that kind of turnover. However he accepted what I had said as the word of the Lord, and made the decision to take out the loan and expand his business. I drove away, praying furiously, and worrying that if the word had not been from God we would be in big trouble. A year later, I visited the man and he was able show me that he was exactly 25 percent up. God did not fail either of us.

In another situation, during the holidays, I was helping my brother-in-law on a job. My role was to climb into a huge duct, polish it, investigate if there was a blockage and clear it. I discovered that the blockage was actually a round piece of aluminium that was designed to open and close. It had broken off at the sides and was now jammed shut. I removed the piece and in doing so noted that, even if it was functioning correctly, it could only ever open a third of the way. The design flaw was affecting the suction through the duct. I asked the Lord to show me how it could be designed to allow maximum

flow. Having received that information, I went to the boss and explained God's idea to him. He sent me to the fitter and turner with this design. However, because I was 'only a cleaner' the fitter very rudely told me where to go. I advised him to ring the boss. The boss told him to do what I said. Initially the fitter wasn't happy, but when I explained the adjustments he became interested. Sure enough, when the adjustments were made, the air began to go full flow. The fitter then asked me if I was really a cleaner. I told him that in fact I was a pastor and explained that God had shown me the design. He had to admit that it was ingenious, but still scoffed at me.
Ps Geoff Wiklund *(Senior Pastor)*

At one point I was working as an electrician for a small electrical company in Auckland.

One day I was given a job to fix a stove out in West Auckland. I quickly grabbed the job card, which had the address on it, jumped into my van and headed for the location.

I normally had a map book in my van so when I got out towards the area where I thought the job was, I stopped and started looking for the book – only to find it wasn't in the van. Oops! 'What do I do now?' I thought. This was before the days of mobile phones and I didn't have a radio telephone in the vehicle.

I hadn't long been baptised in the Holy Spirit and I believed that God not only knew everything about my life as a Christian, but was interested in every part of my life.

'Oh well,' I thought, 'God knows where this place is.' So I simply asked Him to direct me. I started driving again and came to a corner. I asked God which way to go. 'Straight ahead, left or right?' I was moving along, so had to listen to God's Spirit carefully and quickly.

I heard in my spirit, 'Go left, go right, straight ahead, next left ...' and – would you believe it? – when I came around the final corner, there on the right was the street where the job was located. This may sound a bit corny and strange, but it actually happened just like that.

Did I stop carrying a map book and did it ever happen again? No, but God taught me that there is nothing He doesn't know. If we ask Him, He will tell us.

Some years later, I started working for myself. I had been asked to put an additional wall light in a lady's lounge. She told me where she would like it placed.

The job involved finding a wall stud for the light fitting to be screwed into, then getting some wiring up through the wall cavity and down to an existing wall switch.

'Simple,' I thought. To save time, I decided to drill through the stud on an angle to get into the cavity, then go up into the ceiling, drill down through the top plate into the cavity, drop a chain down the wall, hook it out through the hole in the stud,

then pull the wire up with the chain. Simple – I'd done it heaps of times before.

Just before I began drilling, it occurred to me to ask God which side of the stud I should drill out through. To the left or to the right? At this stage I hadn't even been up in the ceiling to see what was there.

Clear as a bell I sensed in my spirit, 'Go to the left', so I did.

When I got up in the ceiling, I found a massive beam sitting on top of the stud. This beam stopped short at the stud, meaning that if I had drilled to the right I would have had to drill down through the big beam and the top plate – there wasn't enough room to work a drill and long bit between the top of the beam and the roof.

Because I had drilled to the left and the beam stopped at the stud, I had only to drill with a short drill through the top plate!

God is interested in everything I do because He's my Father and I'm His son and He never stops loving me. He never says, 'That's too trivial, work it out yourself.' Instead, as I use my brain and plan things, I hear His Spirit talking to me and giving me wisdom and insight along the way. Truly, God is good – all the time.
Brian Vincent *(Retired Electrician)*

Normally I carry my bank card in my purse. Recently I went to pay for my groceries only to find it wasn't there. Fortunately I had another backup card so was able to pay. I looked and looked for the missing card, and finally I asked the Lord where it was. By an impression, He directed me to a small wallet I use when the purse is too big for some outings, and there was my bank card.

On another occasion I couldn't find my shoes and I was flying out to Hawaii the next day. I unpacked my bag – still no shoes. I asked the Lord where they were, but I went to bed that night still not knowing. At 3 am I woke up to an audible voice saying they were in the hot water cupboard wrapped up in my work uniform. And sure enough, there they were. It had been a distinct word of knowledge.

I was talking to a friend on the phone one day, and she told me that her husband was really ill with the flu. Later, as I was cleaning windows, the Holy Spirit prompted me to ring her again. As I did the Holy Spirit showed me how to pray for her husband. He was back at work the next morning.

There are countless times when I have lost things around the home when I was working and in a hurry. I would ask God and He would tell me where they were. Sometimes He would get me to look first, and it could be a waiting game, but there are always things to be learnt.
Lesley Lillie *(Homemaker)*

Life can be varied for an at-home mum – from the mundane of housework to the fun and excitement of watching your young children grow into teenagers and then adults. I can only be grateful to God that in my calling as a mother He has shown me and helped me with many things by His Holy Spirit.

As with most households, life is not always easy or quiet. The calming of arguments either by a word of knowledge or of wisdom, or the gentle reminding of God's grace, has been of use over the years in different situations as our children have grown. In times of uncertainty about health or finances, I have learnt, and still am learning, that He really does know our needs no matter how mundane I may feel they are. God takes an interest. Whether I need an energy boost to help me get things done or courage to face difficulties, or to find something I have misplaced, I just need to take a moment to ask, and surrender the situation to Jesus. When I have done this in these situations, I have found His Holy Spirit is always there to guide, teach or give a word of wisdom or of knowledge.

With His guiding, and by learning to trust Him more and more, I feel His peace and see His hand at work as He reveals His plan and a way through each circumstance.
Julie Samsom *(Homemaker)*

These are examples of the gifts of the Spirit operating in the workplace. Of course, one of the most significant gifts that has not yet been mentioned is healing, and that can be used in the workplace too – but be wise as to where and how. I talk more about that gift below.

THE GIFTS IN THE MARKETPLACE

The gifts of the Spirit can be utilised in all the spaces beyond the walls of the church. This wonderful testimony from a friend of mine named Denis Stewart is an example of how this can happen:

A few months ago I had an appointment at a medical centre in a big mall in the area where I live. As I left to go outside after the appointment, a guy I had never met before, suddenly caught my attention. We seemed to 'eyeball' each other and struck up a conversation. It was strange how it happened so quickly. The Holy Spirit showed me He wanted to use me with something special, so this man and I quickly got onto to talking about the things I was involved with at Charisma Ministries. I had seen people healed of many kinds of aches and pains. The man explained to me he had very sore knees, so I asked him if he would let me lay hands on his knees for healing, which he allowed me to do.

The man's knees were not only healed but through this I was able to share with him how much the Lord loved him and had a great plan for his life. Yes, the door was opened for him to receive Jesus Christ as his personal Saviour!

This testimony is similar to a number of experiences I have had using the gifts of the Holy Spirit in the marketplace. I believe that we are all called to marketplace ministry. Like the example above, stories are the best way to illustrate how this happens. So here are some everyday examples from my life ...

One day I went to a new hairdresser for a haircut. While we were chatting she told me that she had a chest infection or virus of some kind; she'd had it for months and it wouldn't go away. As I was paying, I asked if I could pray for the healing of her infection. She said yes. When I returned a few weeks later I found she had forgotten that she'd ever had a chest problem; the infection had cleared up completely. Then she and I had a conversation about God.

A friend of a family member, a Jewish lady, asked what I was doing these days. I told her that I prayed for sick people. 'Oh,' she says jokingly, 'you should pray for me – I've had a bad neck for a long time.' With cheerful scepticism she let me pray. 'I'm going to ask the Resurrected Jew to heal your neck,' I said. And He did – on the spot. She won't credit the healing to Jesus, concluding instead that I have 'blessed hands', but a seed is sown.

When I was out of town, I visited a friend of a family member. I didn't know her very well, but I said, 'You look stressed and upset; are you OK?' 'Oh,' she replied, 'thank you for noticing.' 'Can I pray for you?' I ask. 'Oh yes please.' Next thing she was sobbing on my chest, and a lapsed Christian was reconnected to God.

In New Caledonia, my wife and I visited a man I hardly knew. As we were leaving he complained about a sore leg which he'd had for quite a while. I offered to pray and he agreed. He was healed on the spot. Some months later the same man said he wanted to give up smoking. I prayed for his deliverance and, when I saw him the next day, he said the urge to smoke had left him.

A neighbour came around to our house one evening. Normally she was a keen walker, but she was having to drive everywhere because she had a ruptured tendon, or something like that. As I heard about this I asked, 'Can I pray for your foot?' She was into New Age ideas and her response was reluctant. 'Mmmm; okay.' I said a prayer and then got her to walk around. The foot was much better. I prayed again before we parted and she left our house walking normally.

I was in Fiji with a ministry friend. We went into a shop and chatted with a woman there. As we talked, she told me she had a lump in her abdomen. My female companion felt the area; the lump was huge! We asked if we could pray. The woman was desperate for help and said yes. *The lump disappeared.*

In Adelaide, Australia, I was leaving the café on the summit of Mount Lofty when a lady entered, pushing a walker. She was with her husband and they were part of a tour group. On an impulse I asked her if she had a sore leg. 'No,' she replied, 'it's my back.' I asked if I could pray for it but she wasn't too sure. I tried to persuade her. 'Okay,' she finally agreed. I prayed and then asked her to put the walker aside and put faith into action. 'How's your back?' I asked. 'It's a little better,' she said. So I prayed again, 'More power, Jesus.' Suddenly, with a look of surprise, she said, *I can stand up straight and the pain's gone!* I had to rejoin my friends who were waiting for me. She and her husband rejoined their group. I wonder what she said to them.

I could go on and on with stories like this. It's wonderful how the Holy Spirit works.

Do I get scared in these situations? Yes I do – I'm not good at breaking the ice with a stranger, although I'm getting better. I remember sitting in a café one day in Anse Vata, Noumea. I'd finished breakfast and was settling down to do the sudoku. Looking across I saw a homeless man on a bench outside. He's slept there all night, and I had noticed him before. I felt I should do something.

I didn't want to. Besides my French isn't very good. What would I say? I tried to focus on the sudoku. But again I got a prompting to do something. So I stood up and bought a croissant. I crossed the road and hovered in the vicinity of the bench. Eventually I caught the man's eye. 'Are you hungry?' I asked in my basic French. I walked over and gave him the croissant. I tried to have a conversation with him, and I thought he was saying he couldn't work because of a shoulder or heart problem. 'I'm a New Zealander and a Christian, can I pray for you?' I said. He said yes so I prayed and then asked, 'How's the shoulder?' 'The pain is gone, it's good,' he replied. I shook his hand, gave him some money and then went on my way.

Does everyone get healed? No. But I believe everyone gets something from God. Some cancer sufferers I have prayed for have come to know the greatest healing of all: salvation. They haven't got what we prayed for but they got Jesus, which is far more important.

In the beginning I saw very few healings. But I persevered and still do. I got some training in Christian healing and deliverance, and hung out with people who had healing ministries. These things made a big difference, after all, Jesus trained His disciples before sending them out.

The number one key is to remember Who we are carrying inside us. We take the Holy Spirit with us wherever we go; the power that raised Jesus from the dead is inside us. The Holy Spirit wants to be made known through us. He is waiting for us to release Him, in Jesus' name. We are the gateways through which God gives out His love and power. He is relying on us.

God, stir us up to go out into the marketplace – outside the walls of our churches – where men, women and children are in need. And that we go in the might of the Holy Spirit, as channels of His mighty gifts, to help our desperately needy world. In Jesus' name. Amen.

HOW TO BECOME A CHRISTIAN

This little book was written for Christians. By 'Christians', I don't just mean people who live good lives. I mean people who are born again by the Spirit of God and who love and follow Jesus Christ.

People are made in three parts: spirit, soul and body. The spirit part was designed to know and commune with a holy God, who is Spirit. Humans were made for intimacy with God, spirit to Spirit. However, human sin separates us from God, resulting in the death of our spirit and loss of communion with God.

Consequently, people tend to operate out of their souls and bodies only. The soul comprises the intellect, the will and the emotions. The result of this is only too apparent in the world: selfishness, pride, greed, hunger, wars, and lack of true peace and meaning.

But God had a plan to redeem humankind. God the Father sent His Son, Jesus, who is also God, to come to earth as a man to show us what God was like – *'if you have seen Me you have seen the Father'* – and to take upon Himself the consequences of our sin. His horrible death on the cross was planned from the very beginning and was predicted in detail in the Old Testament. He paid the price for humankind's sin. Divine justice was satisfied.

But then God raised Jesus from the dead. Jesus promises that those who believe in Him will also be raised from the dead to spend eternity with Him. He gives us His Spirit *now*, as a guarantee, so that we would know Him and walk with Him for the remainder of our earthly lives.

So there we have the essence of the gospel of Jesus Christ. If you acknowledge and confess your sin, if you believe that Jesus took your punishment upon Himself on the cross and that He was raised from the dead, then His righteousness will be imputed to you. God will send His Holy Spirit to regenerate your human spirit – that's what it means to be born again – and you will be able to begin to know and commune with God intimately – which is why He created you in the first place! When your physical body dies, Christ will raise you up and give you a glorious, imperishable one. Wow!

While you continue on this earth, the Holy Spirit (who is also God) will work *in* you (to clean you up and make you more like Jesus in character) and *through* you (to be a blessing to others).

Those who choose not to receive what Jesus paid for will go to judgement with all its consequences. You don't want that.

Here is a prayer you can pray. If you pray it sincerely you will be born again.

Dear God in heaven, I come to You in the name of Jesus. I acknowledge to You that I am a sinner. (Confess all your known sins.) I am truly sorry for my sins and the life that I have lived without You and I need Your forgiveness.

I believe that Your only Son, Jesus Christ, shed His precious blood on the cross and died for my sins, and I am now willing to turn from my sin.

You said in the Bible (Romans 10:9) that if we declare that Jesus is Lord and believe in our hearts that God raised Jesus from the dead, we shall be saved.

Right now I confess Jesus as the Lord of my soul. I believe that God raised Jesus from the dead. This very moment I accept Jesus Christ as my own personal Saviour and, according to His Word, right now I am saved. Thank You, Lord, for loving me so much that You were willing to die in my place. You are amazing, Jesus, and I love you.

Now I ask You to help me by Your Spirit to be the person that You purposed for me to be from before the beginning of time. Lead me to fellow believers and the church of Your choice that I might grow in You. In Jesus' name. Amen.

ABOUT THE AUTHOR

Richard Brunton was a pioneer of the market research industry in New Zealand. He co-founded Colmar Brunton in 1981 and built the business into the country's best known and most trusted research company – www.colmarbrunton.co.nz

He was the driving force behind Colmar Brunton's *'Better Business, Better World'* campaign – a personal crusade around creating profit by creating purpose, or making money by making meaning. He believes (with the research to back it) that organisations that are driven by the big ideal of making their customers' lives better create more shareholder value in the long run than those who focus on other aims.

His articles, speeches and unique perspectives have been published in many magazines and newspapers. Richard was inducted into the Marketing Hall of Fame in 2005, and became a life member of the Marketing

Research Society of New Zealand in 2010. In 2014, he retired as Executive Chairman of Colmar Brunton and has devoted his time to writing, speaking and marketplace ministry.

Richards recently published booklet *The Awesome Power of Blessing* is having a significant impact on the lives of people around the world. The booklet can be downloaded free at:
www.richardbruntonministries.org

Richard attends FaithPointe church in Auckland. He is also a member of the ministry team at Charisma Christian Ministries and teaches in their School of Supernatural Ministry.

He has been married to Nicole for 10 years, has learnt to speak French, and spends time between New Zealand and New Caledonia. He is a keen boatie and fisherman, and owns an amphibious Sealegs boat.

Thanks for reading this little book.

I would love to receive testimonies on how it has changed you, your work, your marketplace ministry or those you may have given it too.

Please contact me via:
richard@richardbruntonministries.org

and visit
www.richardbruntonministries.org